Pocket Guide to Pink Depression Era Glass

Monica Lynn Clements & Patricia Rosser Clements

W9-DFV-799

Schiffer Publishing Ltd

4880 Lower Valley Road, Atglen, PA 19310 USA

Designed by "Sue"
Typeset in ShelleyAllegro BT/ZapfHumnst BT

ISBN: 0-7643-1008-9
Printed in China
1 2 3 4

Published by Schiffer Publishing Ltd.
4880 Lower Valley Road
Atglen, PA 19310
Phone: (610) 593-1777; Fax: (610) 593-2002
e-mail: schifferbk@aol.com
Please visit our website catalog at
www.schifferbooks.com
or write for a free printed catalog.
This book may be purchased from the publisher.
Please include $3.95 for shipping.

In Europe, Schiffer books are distributed by
Bushwood Books
6 Marksbury Avenue
Kew Gardens
Surrey TW9 4JF England
Phone: 44 (0)181 392-8585; Fax: 44 (0)181 392-9876
e-mail: bushwd@aol.com

Please try your bookstore first.

We are interested in hearing from authors
with book ideas on related subjects.

Dedication

For Ollie Tennie Clements

Acknowledgments

Our special thanks goes to each of the contributors: Sharon Ainsworth, Iris Bohanon, Emily Bonner, Joan Stewart Creech, Judith Merritt Davis, Mary Jim Davis, Mary Ellen DeLaughter, Martha Forrest, Mary Ellen Dumas Guinn, Arnie Hays, Pat Henry of Yesterday's Rose, Sarah Lee, Betty LeGrand, Sue Lester, Margaret McRaney, Mary G. Moon, Rebekah Sirmans, J. Marie Taylor, Three Rivers Antiques of Jefferson, Texas, Bea Tipton, and Deanna Young.

As always, our gratitude goes to Mary G. Moon for her guidance and expertise.

Contents

Introduction

The term *depression glass* originated in the 1970s as a way to identify glass made inexpensively during the years of the Great Depression. The meaning of this term has widened extensively, but for the purposes of this book, we have concentrated on the glass made from the late 1920s into the 1940s. Along with the traditional patterns, other pieces produced during the Depression Era are included in the last chapter. Among this glass are examples of elegant glassware.

At one time, Depression Era glass was plentiful. Today, the glass in every color has become scarce or very expensive. Therefore, many collectors look to reproductions to complete their sets or as pieces to use until they can locate the original pieces. For the patterns in which reproduction pieces have been made, a note is included to alert collectors.

Of all the glass made during the Depression Era, the most popular color was pink. Evidence of this fact can be seen in the following pages. We hope you will also enjoy the beauty of pink Depression Era glass.

The purpose of this book is not to set prices but to be used as a guide.

Chapter One: *History*

The Great Depression

The Depression Era refers to the time in American history from 1929 to 1940. The Great Depression officially began on October 24, 1929, known as Black Tuesday, when the stock market collapsed. The result was financial ruin and panic that ran rampant.

Failed businesses and banks along with widespread unemployment devastated the economy for many years. The value of money had fallen and the need for goods declined. Perhaps the hardest hit were the farmers since there was no demand for what they produced. The mainstay of agriculture was demolished by the drought of the 1930s and the tragedy of the Great Plains Dust Bowl.

When Franklin Delano Roosevelt became president, the situation began to change. He came up with the idea for the New Deal and formed agencies to provide ways to help people out of their poverty. While Roosevelt's ideas changed people's lives and ensured that such a catastrophe would never happen again, it wasn't until World War II, with the need for new industry, that the problems caused by the Great Depression were solved completely.

Depression Era Glassware

In order to survive during the years of the Great Depression, glass companies turned to machines and came up with a way to mass produce glassware. The inexpensive formula for the glass included lime, silica, and soda ash.

Glass companies discovered several methods by which they produced Depression Era glass: chipped-mold, paste-mold, cut-mold, and mold-etched glass. Of these, the most popular and the most common way of fashioning glass was the chipped-mold method. This process involved a workman taking an iron mold and etching the design into the mold. After the glass had been placed into the mold, the result was a raised pattern. An advantage to using the chipped-mold method was that the raised design often hid the flaws of bubbles in the glass.

During the Depression Era, the companies which offered lines considered as elegant glass now turned to providing new items for American tables. For example, breakfast sets, bridge sets, luncheon sets, and other pieces such as the sandwich tray became common.

Companies worked to market the inexpensive glass through premiums and promotions. For example, buying a box of oatmeal or cornflakes could ensure that there would be a dish inside the box. Going to the movies could also provide a way to win glassware through a drawing. Other avenues for offering glass included magazine subscriptions.

Out of the array of colors available to consumers in the Depression Era patterns, pink was the most popular. Companies offered patterns that contained pink pieces. Never had the color sounded more glamorous with names such as Cheri-Glo, Flamingo, Nu-Rose, Rose, Rose Glow, Rose Marie, Rose Pink, Rose Tint, and Wild Rose, among others.

Today, the pink dishes have retained their popularity. As pink Depression Era glass becomes harder to find, many collectors are willing to pay the high prices to complete their collections.

Depression Era Glass Companies

Anchor Hocking Glass Company

What began as the Hocking Glass Company in the early 1900s became the Anchor Hocking Glass Company in 1937. The merging of Anchor Cap and Closure Corporation, its subsidiaries, and the Hocking Glass Company heralded the beginning of a strong force in the production of glassware.

With plants in Canada, New Jersey, New York, and Pennsylvania, the company continued to expand its base through the acquisition of Maywood Glass Company and the Carr-Lowrey Glass Company in the 1940s. Through these companies, Anchor Hocking entered into toiletries and cosmetic containers production.

Oyster and Pearl relish dish.

Anchor Hocking continued with its wide ranging production of glassware that began during the Hocking Glass Company years. The company still produces glassware of durable quality. For the purposes of this book, the Manhattan pattern and Oyster and Pearl patterns are included as representatives of Anchor Hocking's top notch glassware production.

Federal Glass Company

Located in Columbus, Ohio, the Federal Glass Company was considered an innovative company that thrived into the late 1970s. The manufacture of affordable glassware began in the early 1900s. Like other companies, Federal Glass Company created patterns using the old fashioned method of hand pressing. With the demand of consumers, the company turned to machines and soon made colored glass using machine pressed methods.

The mold-etched method was used to create such patterns as Columbia, Georgian, Normandie, Parrot, Patrician, and Sharon. During the 1930s, the company utilized the chip-mold method in the creation of Rosemary and Sharon. From the 1930s until the 1940s, the company produced glassware in pink, then known as Rose Glow. Colonial Fluted and Diana (named for G. H. Kuse's daughter) represent other successful pressed patterns that came from the company.

Normandie cup.

Sharon cup.

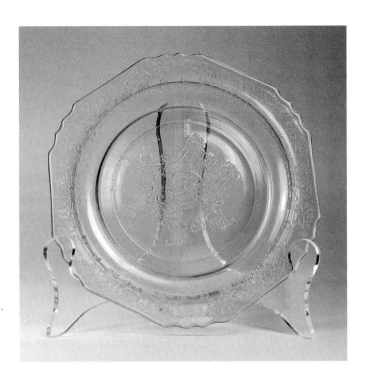

Normandie salad plate.

Left. Sharon vegetable bowl.
Center. Sharon cup and saucer.
Right. Sharon dinner plate.

Fenton Glass Company

Two brothers, Frank Fenton and John Fenton, founded Fenton Glass Company which first appeared in 1906. Famous for its production of carnival glass during the 1920s, the company expanded its designs and began to produce patterns in an array of colors. In 1928, Fenton Glass Company introduced Lincoln Inn, a prominent and popular pattern found in pink.

The success of Fenton Art Glass Company continues today in Williamstown, West Virginia. The family run firm produces fine glass that collectors enjoy in the present day.

Hazel-Atlas Glass Company

One of the most prolific companies that produced glass during the Depression Era was the Hazel-Atlas Glass Company. Perhaps this was due to the fact that the company operated several plants in Oklahoma, Pennsylvania, and West Virginia. In these plants, the company started its production by making containers and fruit jars. During the early 1900s, the West Virginia plant at Clarksburg became the central location where the manufacture of tableware began.

The myriad of patterns of Depression Era glass produced by Hazel-Atlas in pink includes Aurora, Cloverleaf, Colonial Block, Florentine No. 1, Florentine No. 2, Fruits, Moderntone, New Century, Ribbon, Royal Lace, and Starlight. Kitchenware items and a wide selection of glasses, pitchers, and the like also came from Hazel-Atlas. The color of Sunset pink appeared in the early 1930s.

Three Florentine No. 1 berry bowls.

Hocking Glass Company

Issac J. Collins was the mastermind behind the Hocking Glass Company. He assembled eight investors and enlisted the help of E. B. Good to purchase a glass company in Lancaster, Ohio. The company was renamed Hocking Glass Company because of its close proximity to the Hocking River.

With fifty employees, the Hocking Glass Company began its operation in 1905. Under Collins, the company flourished. A fire destroyed the company in 1924, and instead of signaling the end of the company, a new factory was built. The new factory devoted itself to the production of glassware. Six months after the fire, Hocking Glass Company was stronger than ever having obtained controlling interest in two companies: the Lancaster Glass Company and the Standard Glass Manufacturing Company.

During the 1920s, Hocking became known for its innovative production of glassware through the use of technology. Their creation was a machine that had fifteen molds and manufactured ninety pieces of glass a minute. This innovation allowed Hocking Glass Company to thrive during a time when other companies struggled to stay in business or failed.

Hocking Glass Company items are in abundance today. The company's pink color, Rose, made its debut in 1926. Hocking installed pink tanks in the early 1930s. The number of important patterns in Depression Era glass were evidence that the company was prolific in glassware manufacture. Block Optic, Cameo, Circle, Colonial, Coronation, Fire-King Philbe, Fortune, Mayfair, Miss America, Old Café, Old Colony, Princess, Queen Mary, Roulette, Spiral, and Waterford are the patterns found in pink.

Fortune cup and saucer.

Fortune berry bowl.

Mayfair cookie jar.

Front left. Old Colony salad plate.
Front center left. Old Colony saucer.
Center. Old Colony comport.
Right. Old Colony cereal bowl.
Back left. Old Colony divided platter.
Back right. Old Colony dinner plate.

Left. Miss America footed creamer.
Center. Miss America footed salt and pepper shakers.
Right. Miss America footed sugar.

Below:
Left. Queen Mary large berry bowl.
Right. Queen Mary berry bowl.

Waterford
platter.

Imperial Glass Corporation

A company associated with the making of iridescent glass was the Imperial Glass Corporation. This company's founder was Edward Muhleman. In 1904, the company began its manufacturing of glass and would continue for the next eighty years. During the 1930s, Imperial bought the molds from the Central Glass Company. Later, Imperial would purchase Heisey Company and Cambridge Glass Company.

Imperial produced a wide variety of designs in iridescent blown and pressed glass. The company dabbled in Depression Era glass patterns. Those patterns available in pink are Beaded Block, Diamond Quilted (also known as "Flat Diamond"), and Twisted Optic. By the 1920s, Imperial had introduced its pink color called Rose Marie. Later, the color became known simply as Rose.

Indiana Glass Company

Located in Dunkirk, Indiana, the Indiana Glass Company began in 1904 and continues to produce glass in the present day. Early advertisements from the company boasted its manufacture of goblets, lamps, soda fountain supplies, and tableware. During the 1920s and 1930s, the company produced several Depression Era patterns including the durable and distinctive Tea Room. The company called its pink color Rose.

Jeannette Glass Company

The Jeannette Glass Company originated in the late 1890s. By the 1920s, the company had turned to machinery for prodution of its glassware. Through the years Jeannette Glass Company manufactured tableware, novelty items, candy containers, and kitchenware. For many years, the main colors of glass coming from this company were pink and green.

The company described the color of its pink tableware as Wild Rose. Cube (also called "Cubist") marked the beginning of the production of pink Depression Era tableware. This pattern was a pressed pattern. The pressed patterns remained favorites with Anniversary, Holiday, Homepsun, Sierra, Swirl, and Windsor. The company followed with etched glass patterns such as Cherry Blossom and Floral.

Holiday cup and saucer.

Left. Homespun 4 oz. footed tumbler.
Center left. Homespun bowl and sherbet plate.
Center right. Homespun cup and saucer.
Right. Homespun 15 oz. footed tumbler.
Back center. Homespun dinner plate.

Left. Sierra cereal bowl.
Center. Sierra dinner plate.
Right. Sierra cup and saucer.

Left. Sierra two-handled serving tray.
Center. Sierra large berry bowl.
Right. Sierra oval platter.

Swirl candy dish.

Windsor berry bowl.

Cherry Blossom cup.

Cherry Blossom round berry bowl.

While all the aforementioned patterns come in pink, other patterns found in the pink color are Adam, Doric, Doric and Pansy, Hex Optic, Iris and Herringbone, Sierra, and Sunflower.

Adam candy dish with cover.

Pair of Adam candlesticks.

Adam cup and saucer.

Below:
Left. Adam sugar with lid.
Center. Adam salt and pepper shakers.
Right. Adam creamer.

Lancaster Glass Company

In the early 1900s, the father and son team of Lucien B. Martin and L. Phillip Martin started the Lancaster Glass Company in Lancaster, Ohio. The company began producing fine vases in 1909, and from there moved into the manufacture of tableware and novelties, including animal figures.

The Lancaster Glass Company produced two stylish patterns of Depression Era glass in pink during the 1930s. Jubilee with its etched flowers and Patrick with its design of clustered flowers share the same shapes in many of the pieces.

Liberty Works

With the leadership of John E. Marsden, Liberty Works started out as Liberty Cut Glass Works in 1902. During the 1920s, an addition onto the plant provided the means to manufacture glass in an array of colors. The company devoted one tank primarily for making pink glass, a color which the company referred to as Rose Glass.

The standouts in the patterns offered in pink were American Pioneer and the distinctive shapes found in the Octagon Optic line.

Macbeth-Evans Glass Company

During the years of the Depression, the Macbeth-Evans Company favored the production of pink glass. The glassware made by this company was often thinner and more delicate than the glass of patterns made by other companies. Unlike other companies, the Macbeth-Evans Company did not manufacture such items as butter dishes, candlesticks, or cookie jars.

In the late 1920s, the company began its Depression Era patterns with the mold-etched pattern Dogwood (also called "Apple Blossom" or "Wild Rose"). Other pink patterns were American Sweetheart, Petalware (shown opposite), S Pattern, and Thistle. The mold from the Dogwood pattern was used in the production of Thistle.

U. S. Glass Company

The United States Glass Company consolidated fifteen glass factories as a way to produce glass in a more efficient way and eliminate competition. Thus, the company began in 1891 to manufacture all kinds of glass items from soda glasses to tableware to novelty items and more.

The zenith of the company's glass production came between 1920 and 1940. Glass in a wide array of colors and styles was created with the company achieving success with its lines of iridescent glass as well as satin glass.

Petalware cereal bowl.

Like other glass companies, U. S. Glass Company manufactured inexpensive glass in different colors.

In the 1920s, the company introduced a color called Old Rose. During the late 1920s and early 1930s, Rose Pink became the term used to describe pink glass. The patterns in pink from this company were Cherryberry, Floral and Diamond Band, Flower Garden with Butterflies (also called "Butterflies and Roses"), Strawberry, and U.S. Swirl.

Westmoreland Glass Company

First known for its novelty items and condiments, the Westmoreland Glass Company located in Grapeville, Pennsylvania, originated in 1890. The company's creations in candy dishes and the like could be found in dime stores, but by the 1920s, the company decided to specialize in glassware. Westmoreland took its glass making seriously and soon had the largest factory where the production and decoration of glass took place.

English Hobnail, a hand molded pattern, with its characteristic bumps proved a popular design. In 1926, the company introduced its pink color, Rose. This color was also known as Roselin.

Chapter Two: *Depression Era Patterns*

Adam

Made by Jeannette Glass Company from 1932 to 1934.

Ashtray, 4.5"	$30-32
Bowl, berry, 4.75"	$17-19
Bowl, cereal, 5.75"	$42-44
Bowl, covered, 9"	$58-60
Bowl, oval, 10"	$32-35
Bowl, 9.5"	$32-34
Butter dish with cover	$87-89
Footed cake plate, 10"	$30-32
Pair of candlesticks, 4"	$94-96
Candy dish and cover, 2.5"	$97-99

Coaster, 3.75"	$24-26
Creamer	$22-24
Cup	$27-29
Pitcher, 32 oz.	$42-44
Plate, sherbet, 6"	$11-13
Plate, square salad, 7.75"	$17-19
Plate, square dinner, 9"	$37-39
Plate, grill, 9"	$22-24
Platter, 11.75"	$32-34
Saucer, 6"	$7-8
Sherbet, 3"	$32-34
Sugar	$19-22
Sugar or candy cover	$27-29
Tumbler, 4.5"	$34-36
Tumbler, 5.5"	$67-69

Note: Reproductions of the butter dish and lid have been manufactured.

American Sweetheart

Made by MacBeth-Evans Glass Company from 1930 to 1936.

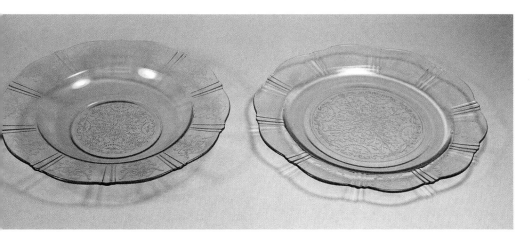

Bowl, berry, 3.75"	$72-78
Bowl, cream soup, 4.5"	$85-92
Bowl, cereal, 6"	$22-24
Bowl, round berry, 9"	$53-58
Bowl, flat soup, 9.5"	$73-79
Bowl, vegetable, 11"	$68-73
Creamer, footed	$17-19
Cup	$22-24
Plate, bread and butter, 6"	$7-9
Plate, salad, 8"	$13-15
Plate, dinner, 9.75"	$41-45
Plate, salver, 12"	$24-28
Platter, 13"	$57-63
Saucer	$6-8
Sherbet, footed, 3.75"	$25-28
Sherbet, footed, 4.25	$22-26
Sugar, open, footed	$14-16
Tumbler, 5 oz., 3.5"	$97-99
Tumbler, 9 oz., 4.25"	$83-85
Tumbler, 10 oz., 4.75"	$120-130

Anniversary

Made by Jeannette Glass Company during the late 1940s.

Bowl, berry, 4.88"	$9-12
Bowl, soup, 7.38"	$19-21
Butter dish and cover	$57-59
Cake plate, 12.5"	$47-49
Creamer	$12-14
Cup	$10-12
Plate, sherbet, 6.25"	$5-7
Plate, dinner, 9"	$16-18
Saucer	$4-6
Sherbet	$11-13
Sugar	$11-13
Sugar lid	$13-15

Block Optic ("Block")

Made by Hocking Glass Company from 1929 to 1933.

Bowl, berry, 4.25"	$14-16
Bowl, cereal, 5.25"	$30-32
Bowl, salad, 7.25"	$165-167
Bowl, berry, 8.5"	$37-39
Butter tub (no cover)	$108-120
Candy jar with cover, 2.25"	$57-59
Compote, mayonnaise, 4"	$77-79
Creamer	$16-18
Cup	$9-12
Pitcher, 54 oz., 7.63"	$127-129
Pitcher, 54 oz., 8.5"	$52-54
Pitcher, 80 oz., 8"	$92-94
Plate, sherbet, 6"	$4-6
Plate, luncheon, 8"	$7-9
Plate, dinner, 9"	$42-44
Footed salt and pepper	$82-84
Saucer	$10-12
Sherbet, 5.5 oz, 3.75"	$9-11
Sherbet, 6 oz., 4.75"	$19-22
Sugar	$14-16
Tumbler, 5 oz., 3.5"	$24-25
Tumbler, footed, 3 oz., 3.5"	$32-35
Tumbler, flat, 9.5 oz.	$17-20
Tumbler, footed, 9 oz.	$17-20
Tumbler, flat, 10 oz.	$20-23
Tumbler, footed, 10 oz.	$34-37
Tumbler, flat, 15 oz.	$40-45

Cherry Blossom

Made by Jeannette Glass Company from 1930 to 1939.

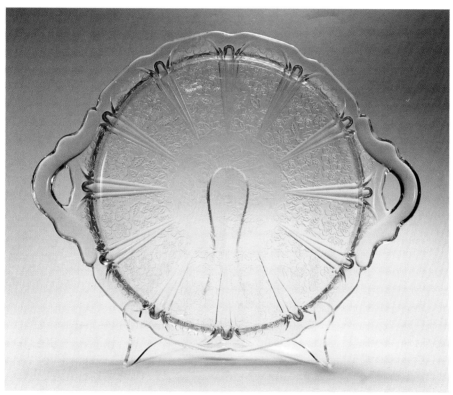

Bowl, berry, 4.75"	$19-22
Bowl, cereal, 5.75"	$52-55
Bowl, soup, 7.75"	$92-96
Bowl, round berry, 8.5"	$52-55
Bowl, vegetable, 9"	$47-52
Bowl, two-handled, 9"	$49-54
Bowl, fruit, 10.5"	$97-102
Butter dish with cover	$87-92
Cake plate, 10.25".	$34-36
Creamer	$24-26
Cup	$24-26
Pitcher scalloped or round bottom, 36 oz., 6.75"	$60-65
Pitcher, footed, 36 oz., 8"	$60-65
Pitcher, flat, 42 oz., 8"	$57-62
Plate, sherbet, 6"	$10-12
Plate, salad, 7"	$24-26
Plate, dinner, 9"	$27-29
Platter, oval, 9"	$875-910
Platter, divided	$72-75
Saucer	$7-9
Sherbet	$20-22
Sugar	$17-19
Sugar cover	$20-22
Tray, two-handled, 10.5"	$32-35
Tumbler, footed, 4 oz., 3.75"	$20-22
Tumbler, round, footed, 9 oz., 3.75"	$37-40
Tumbler, scalloped foot, 8 oz., 4.5"	$36-39
Tumbler, flat, 4 oz., 3.5"	$22-24
Tumbler, flat, 9 oz., 4.25	$20-22
Tumbler, flat, 12 oz., 5"	$62-66

Note: During the 1970s, reproduction dishes began to appear on the market.

Child's Junior Dinner Set

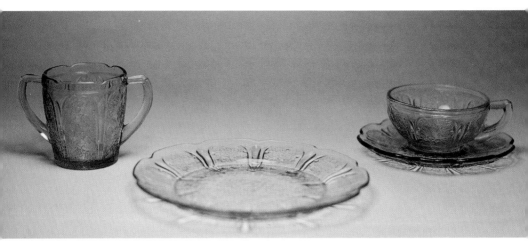

Cherry Blossom children's dishes.

Entire 14-piece set	$364-398
Creamer	$52-55
Cup	$42-45
Plate	$14-16
Saucer	$9-11
Sugar	$52-55

Cloverleaf

Made by Hazel-Atlas Glass Company from 1930 to 1936.

Bowl, dessert, 4"	$17-19
Cup	$9-11
Plate, luncheon, 8"	$9-13
Saucer	$6-8
Sherbet, footed	$12-14

Colonial ("Knife and Fork")

Made by Hocking Glass Company from 1934 to 1938.

Bowl, 3.75"	$52-55
Bowl, berry, 4.5"	$18-21
Bowl, cereal, 5.5"	$62-66
Bowl, cream soup, 4.5"	$77-82
Bowl, large berry, 9"	$30-33
Bowl, vegetable, 10"	$37-41
Creamer, 8 oz., 5"	$62-67
Cup	$14-16
Plate, sherbet	$8-10
Plate, luncheon, 8.5"	$11-13
Plate, dinner, 10"	$57-63
Platter, oval, 12"	$35-39
Salt and pepper shakers	$142-149
Saucer	$8-10
Sherbet	$14-16
Sugar, 5"	$27-29
Sugar cover	$62-68
Tumbler, juice, 5 oz., 3"	$22-24
Tumbler, water, 9 oz., 4"	$22-24
Tumbler, iced tea, 12 oz.	$52-57

Colonial Block

Made by Hazel-Atlas Glass Company from late 1920s until the early 1930s.

Bowl, 4″	$8-10
Bowl, 7″	$22-24
Butter dish	$47-52
Butter tub	$47-53
Candy dish and cover, 8.5″	$42-47
Creamer	$14-16
Goblet	$15-17
Pitcher	$47-53
Sherbet	$12-14
Sugar	$12-14
Sugar cover	$14-16

Coronation ("Banded Fine Rib" or "Saxon")

Made by the Hocking Glass Company from 1936 to 1940.

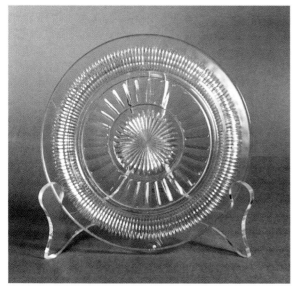

Bowl, berry, 4.25"	$7-9
Bowl, nappy, 6.5"	$8-10
Bowl, large berry, 8"	$11-13
Cup	$8-10
Pitcher, 68 oz., 7.75"	$525-555
Plate, sherbet, 6"	$4-6
Plate, luncheon, 8.5"	$7-9
Saucer	$4-6
Sherbet	$7-9
Tumbler, footed, 10 oz., 5"	$35-39

Cube ("Cubist")

Made by the Jeannette Glass Company from 1929 to 1933.

Bowl, dessert, 4.5"	$9-11
Bowl, 4.5"	$10-12
Bowl, salad, 6.5"	$12-14
Butter dish and cover	$67-73
Candy jar and cover, 6.5"	$32-38
Creamer, 2.63"	$9-11
Creamer, 3.24"	$8-10
Cup	$9-11
Pitcher, 45 oz., 8.75"	$200-225
Plate, sherbet, 6"	$5-7
Plate, luncheon, 8"	$8-10
Salt and pepper	$37-39
Saucer	$5-7
Sherbet	$9-11
Sugar, 2"	$4-6

Sugar, 3"	$9-11
Sugar or candy cover	$17-19
Tumbler, 9 oz., 4"	$68-74

Diamond Quilted ("Flat Diamond")

Made by the Imperial Glass Company from the late 1920s to the early 1930s.

Bowl with handle, 5.5"	$9.50-10.50
Pair of candlesticks	$24-28
Candy jar with cover	$66-75
Cup	$8-10
Plate, lunch, 8"	$13-15
Sherbet	$7-9
Sugar	$15-17

Diana

Made by the Federal Glass Company from 1937 to 1941.

Bowl, cereal, 5"	$12-14
Bowl, cream soup, 5.5"	$27-31
Bowl, salad, 7"	$22-24
Bowl, console fruit, 11"	$42-48
Bowl, scalloped edge, 12"	$32-35
Creamer	$14-16
Cup	$20-22
Plate, bread and butter, 6"	$6-8
Plate, dinner, 9.5"	$18-20
Plate, sandwich, 11.75"	$27-31
Platter, 12"	$30-35
Salt and pepper	$77-82
Saucer	$7-9
Sherbet	$14-16
Sugar, oval, open	$14-16
Tumbler, 9 oz., 4.12"	$47-52

Dogwood ("Apple Blossom" or "Wild Rose")

Made by the MacBeth-Evans Company from 1929 to 1932.

Bowl, cereal, 5.5″	$35-38
Bowl, berry, 8.5″	$64-69
Cake plate, 13″	$132-137
Creamer, 2.5″	$22-24
Creamer, 3.25″	$24-26
Cup	$19-21

Pitcher, 80 oz., with decoration, 8"	$235-245
Plate, bread, 6"	$10-12
Plate, luncheon, 8"	$9-12
Plate, dinner, 9.25"	$40-45
Saucer	$8-10
Sherbet	$40-45
Sugar, 2.5"	$20-22
Sugar, 3.25"	$20-22
Tumbler, 10 oz., decorated, 4"	$42-46
Tumbler, 11 oz, decorated, 4.75"	$47-51
Tumbler, 12 oz., decorated, 5"	$67-72

Doric

Made by the Jeannette Glass Company from 1935 to 1938.

Bowl, berry, 4.5"	$11-13
Bowl, cereal, 5.5"	$67-69
Bowl, large berry, 8.25"	$30-34
Bowl, vegetable, handled, 9"	$20-22
Bowl, vegetable, oval, 9"	$34-37
Butter dish with cover	$72-76
Cake plate with three legs, 10"	$27-30
Candy dish with cover, 8"	$40-45
Creamer, 4"	$14-16
Cup	$9-12
Pitcher, 36 oz., 6"	$40-42
Plate, sherbet, 6"	$6-8
Plate, salad, 7"	$22-25
Plate, dinner, 9"	$18-20
Platter, oval, 12"	$27-31
Salt and pepper	$37-42
Saucer	$5-7
Sherbet, footed	$16-18

Sugar	$14-16
Sugar cover	$16-18
Tray, with handles, 10"	$17-19
Tumbler, flat, 9 oz., 4.5"	$67-72
Tumbler, footed, 10 0z., 4"	$67-72
Tumbler, footed, 12 oz., 5"	$82-87

Doric and Pansy

Made by the Jeannette Glass Company from 1937 to 1938.

Doric and Pansy children's dishes.

Children's Set ("Pretty Polly Party Dishes")

Entire 14-piece set	$298-326
Creamer	$37-39
Cup	$37-39
Plate	$10-12
Saucer	$9-11
Sugar	$37-39

Floral and Diamond Band

Made by U. S. Glass Company from 1927 to 1931.

Bowl, berry, 4.5"	$10-12
Bowl, large berry, 8"	$17-19
Butter dish and cover	$139-145
Creamer, 4.74"	$20-22
Pitcher, 42 oz., 8"	$97-104
Plate, luncheon, 8"	$47-52
Sherbet	$9-11
Sugar, 5.25"	$17-19
Sugar lid	$57-62
Tumbler, water, 4"	$22-24
Tumbler, ice tea, 5"	$42-46

Florentine No. 1 ("Poppy No. 1")

Made by the Hazel-Atlas Glass Company from 1934 to 1936.

Bowl, berry, 5"	$18-22
Bowl, cereal, 6"	$28-30
Berry bowl, large, 8.5"	$38-40
Butter with cover	$165-170
Pitcher, footed, 36 oz., 6.5"	$46-48
Plate, grill, 10"	$20-22
Platter, oval, 11.5"	$23-25
Salt and pepper	$67-69
Sherbet	$12-14
Sugar with cover	$44-46
Creamer	$22-24
Tumbler, water, footed, 9 oz. 5.25"	$27-29

Note: Beware of reproduction salt and pepper shakers.

Fortune

Made by the Hocking Glass Company from 1937 to 1938.

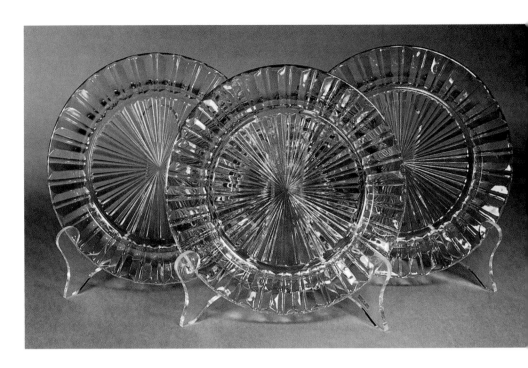

Bowl, berry, 4″	$9-12
Bowl, dessert, 4.5″	$9-11
Bowl, handled, 4.5″	$11-13
Bowl, rolled edge, 5.25″	$14-16
Bowl, large berry, 7.75″	$20-22
Cup	$9-12
Plate, sherbet, 6″	$6-8
Plate, luncheon, 8″	$24-26
Saucer	$5-7
Tumbler, juice, 5 oz., 3.5″	$12-14
Tumbler, water, 9 oz., 4″	$14-16

Hex Optic ("Honeycomb")

Made by the Jeannette Glass Company from 1928 to 1932.

Bowl, berry, ruffled, 4.25"	$8-10
Bowl, berry, 7.25"	$11-13
Butter dish and cover	$80-90
Creamer, with handles	$8-10
Cup	$6-8
Pitcher, 32 oz., 5"	$24-26
Pitcher, footed, 48 oz., 9"	$47-49
Plate, sherbet, 6"	$4-6
Plate, luncheon, 8"	$8-10
Platter, 11"	$17-19
Salt and pepper	$29-31
Saucer	$4-6
Sugar	$8-10
Sugar shaker	$190-200
Sherbet, footed, 5 oz.	$6-8
Tumbler, 9 oz., 3.75"	$6-8
Tumbler, footed, 5.75"	$12-14
Tumbler, footed, 7"	$14-16

Hobnail

Made by the Hocking Glass Company from 1934 to 1936.

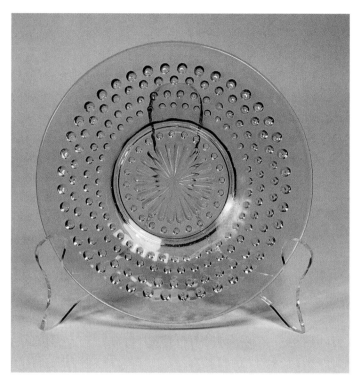

Bowl, cereal, 5.5"	$5-7
Bowl, salad, 7"	$7-9
Cup	$6-8
Creamer (footed)	$6-8
Goblet, water, 10 oz.	$9-12
Goblet, ice tea, 13 oz.	$10-12
Pitcher, milk, 18 oz.	$22-24
Pitcher, 67 oz.	$27-29
Plate, sherbet, 6"	$4-6
Plate, luncheon, 8.5"	$5-7
Saucer	$4-6
Sherbet	$5-7
Sugar (footed)	$6-8
Tumbler, juice, 5 oz.	$6-8
Tumbler, ice tea, 15 oz.	$9-11

Holiday ("Buttons & Bows")

Made by the Jeannette Glass Company from 1947 to 1949.

Bowl, berry, 5.12"	$14-16
Bowl, soup, 7.75"	$57-65
Bowl, large berry, 8.5"	$30-32
Bowl, vegetable, 9.5"	$30-32
Butter dish and cover	$42-47
Cake plate with three legs, 10.5"	$102-112
Creamer	$10-12
Cup (in two sizes)	$10-12
Pitcher, milk, 16 oz., 4.75"	$67-69
Pitcher, 52 oz., 6.75"	$40-45
Plate, sherbet, 6"	$8-10
Plate, dinner, 9"	$19-21
Platter, oval, 11.38"	$22-24
Saucer	$6-8
Sherbet	$8-10
Sugar	$12-14
Sugar cover	$17-19
Tray, sandwich, 10.5"	$19-21
Tumbler, flat, 10 oz., 4"	$24-26
Tumbler, footed, 4"	$47-52
Tumbler, footed, 6"	$155-164

Homespun ("Fine Rib")

Made by Jeannette Glass Company from 1939 to 1940.

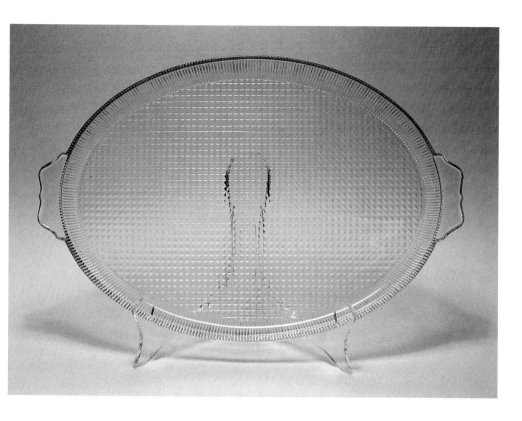

Bowl, with closed handles, 4.5"	$13-15
Bowl, cereal, 5"	$33-36
Bowl, large berry, 8.25"	$24-27
Butter dish and cover	$62-67
Creamer, footed	$12-14
Cup	$12-14
Plate, sherbet, 6"	$8-10
Plate, dinner, 9.25"	$19-21
Platter, 13"	$18-20
Saucer	$6-8
Sherbet	$20-22
Sugar, footed	$11-13
Tumbler, footed, 5 oz., 4"	$9-11
Tumbler, footed, 15 oz., 6.25"	$30-35
Tumbler, footed, 15 oz., 6.38"	$30-35

Child's Tea Set

Homepsun children's dishes.

14-piece set	$380-408
Cup	$37-39
Plate	$15-17
Saucer	$12-14
Teapot	$47-49
Teapot cover	$77-79

Jubilee

Made by the Lancaster Glass Company during the early 1930s.

Bowl, three footed, 5.12" x 8"	$245-265
Bowl, flat fruit, 11.5"	$205-225
Candy jar with lid, three footed	$320-330
Creamer	$37-42
Cup	$38-45
Plate, salad, 7"	$24-26
Plate, luncheon, 8.75"	$29-31
Plate, sandwich, 13.5"	$87-92
Saucer	$14-16
Sugar	$35-41
Tray, cake, 11"	$67-72
Tumbler, water, 10 oz., 6"	$75-79

Lincoln Inn

Made by Fenton Glass Company in the late 1920s.

Bowl, cereal, 6″	$11-13
Candy dish, oval, footed	$22-24
Creamer	$17-19
Cup	$12-14
Goblet, water	$19-21
Goblet, wine	$19-21
Plate, 8″	$9-11
Plate, 12″	$19-21
Saucer	$5-7
Sherbet, 4.74″	$14-16

Madrid

Made by Federal Glass Company from 1932 to 1939.

Reproduction Madrid glasses, ca. 1970s. $8-10 each.

Bowl, vegetable, 10"	$27-29
Cup	$15-18
Plate, relish, 10.25"	$15-20
Plate, sherbet, 6"	$6-8
Plate, salad, 7.5"	$11-13
Plate, luncheon, 8.88"	$10-12
Plate, cake, round, 11.25"	$12-14
Platter, oval, 11.5"	$17-19
Saucer	$7-9
Tumbler, 9 oz., 4.25"	$25-27

Note: Federal Glass Company manufactured new pieces of Madrid as the Recollection line, and the new dishes made their debut in amber during the Bicentennial. Each piece has the small indentation of a "76" on it. When Federal declared bankruptcy, Indiana Glass Company bought the molds, removed the "76", and made the glass in other colors. The pink is extremely pale in comparison to the old pink. The reproduced pink pieces are easy to spot.

Manhattan ("Horizontal Ribbed")
Made by Anchor Hocking Glass Company from 1939 to 1941.

Bowl, cereal, 5.25"	$70-80
Bowl, with closed handles, 8"	$24-26
Bowl, fruit, with open handle, 9.5"	$34-39
Candy dish with three legs	$13-15
Compote, 5.75"	$37-42
Cup	$135-145
Pitcher, tilted, 80 oz.	$67-73
Plate, sherbet, 6"	$52-58
Plate, dinner, 10.25"	$197-210
Salt and pepper	$55-65
Saucer	$47-55
Sherbet	$17-19
Sugar	$13-15
Tumbler, footed, 10 oz.	$19-21

Mayfair ("Open Rose")

Made by Hocking Glass Company from 1931 to 1937.

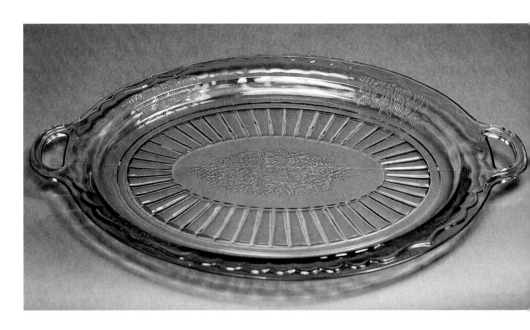

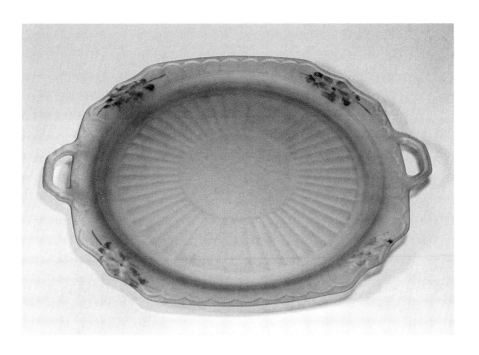

Satin finish cake plate with handles. $38-40.

Bowl, cream soup, 5″	$57-62
Bowl, cereal, 5.5″	$33-32
Bowl, vegetable, 7″	$70-75
Bowl, oval vegetable, 9.5″	$32-36
Bowl, vegetable, 10″	$32-36
Butter dish and cover	$70-76
Cake plate, footed,	$35-38
Candy dish and cover	$57-62
Cookie jar with lid	$57-62
Creamer	$32-37
Cup	$20-22
Goblet, cocktail, 4″	$92-98
Goblet, wine, 4.5″	$97-105
Goblet, water, 5.75″	$72-76
Pitcher, 37 oz., 6″	$57-63
Pitcher, 60 oz., 8″	$57-63
Pitcher, 80 oz., 8.5″	$117-127
Plate, 5.75″	$16-18
Plate, dinner, 9.5″	$55-59
Plate, sherbet, 6.5″	$16-18
Plate, luncheon, 8.5″	$30-35
Plate, dinner, 9.5″	$55-59
Plate, grill, 9.5″	$42-47
Plate, cake with two handles, 12″	$52-56

Sandwich server with handle in center	$50-56
Saucer	$37-42
Tumbler, juice, 9 oz., 3.5"	$47-53
Tumbler, water, 11 oz., 4.75"	$190-202
Tumbler, footed, 10 oz., 5.25"	$47-53
Tumbler, footed, 15 oz., 6.5"	$47-53

Note: Beware of pink reproduction cookie jars, juice pitchers, salt and pepper shakers, and shot glasses.

Miss America

Made by Hocking Glass Company from 1933 to 1937.

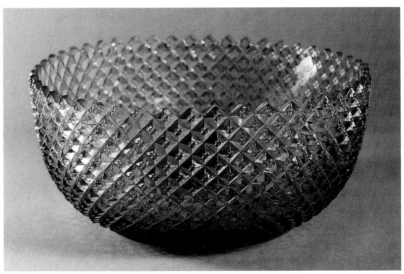

Bowl, berry, 6.25"	$27-30
Bowl, fruit, 8.75"	$67-72
Bowl, oval vegetable, 10"	$32-36
Butter dish and cover	$620-630
Cake plate, footed, 12"	$47-52
Candy jar and cover, 11.5"	$167-177
Celery dish, 10.5"	$35-39
Coaster, 5.75"	$35-39
Compote, 5"	$29-33
Creamer, footed	$22-25
Cup	$27-30
Goblet, wine, 3 oz., 3.75"	$87-93
Goblet, juice, 5 oz., 4.75"	$97-107
Goblet, water, 10 oz., 5.5"	$47-53
Pitcher, 65 oz., 8"	$132-142
Pitcher, 65 oz., lip for ice, 8.5"	$227-235
Plate, sherbet, 5.75"	$13-15
Plate, salad, 8.5"	$25-27
Plate, dinner, 10.5"	$32-36
Plate, grill, 10.25"	$27-32
Platter, oval, 12"	$32-36
Relish, round divided, 11.75"	$450-500
Salt and pepper	$62-67
Saucer	$9-11
Sherbet	$17-19
Sugar	$20-22
Tumbler, juice, 5 oz., 4"	$55-60
Tumbler, water, 10 oz., 4.5"	$35-39
Tumbler, iced tea, 14 oz., 5.75"	$92-102

Note: Beware of the reproduction pieces such as the butter dish and salt and pepper shakers.

New Century

Made by Hazel-Atlas Glass Company from 1930 to 1935.

Cup	$15-17
Pitcher, 60 oz. with or without lip, 7.75"	$37-41
Pitcher, 80 oz., with or without lip, 8"	$44-49
Saucer	$10-12
Tumbler, 5 oz., 3.5"	$20-22
Tumbler, water, 9 oz., 4.25"	$16-22
Tumbler, 10 oz., 5"	$18-24
Tumbler, 12 oz., 5.25"	$26-33

Normandie ("Bouquet and Lattice")

Made by the Federal Glass Company from 1933 to 1940.

Bowl, berry, 5"	$10-12
Bowl, cereal, 6.5"	$35-38
Bowl, large berry, 8.5"	$27-30
Bowl, oval vegetable, 10"	$40-45
Creamer	$14-16
Cup	$12-14

Pitcher, 80 oz., 8"	$160-175
Plate, dinner, 11"	$110-120
Plate, sherbet, 6"	$7-9
Plate, salad, 7.75"	$14-16
Plate, luncheon, 9.25"	$16-18
Saucer	$6-8
Sherbet	$9-12
Sugar	$14-16
Sugar lid	$190-199
Tumbler, juice, 5 oz., 4"	$92-98
Tumbler, water, 9 oz., 4.25"	$57-62
Tumbler, iced tea, 12 oz., 5"	$95-115

Old Café

Made by the Hocking Glass Company from 1936 to 1938 and again in 1940.

Bowl, berry, 3.75" $9-11
Bowl, cereal, 5.5" $17-22
Bowl, 9" $15-18
Cup $9-12

Plate, sherbet, 6"	$5-7
Plate, dinner, 10"	$57-62
Saucer	$5-7
Tumbler, juice, 3"	$14-16
Tumbler, water, 4"	$16-18

Old Colony ("Lace Edge")

Made by the Hocking Glass Company from 1935 to 1938.

Left. Satin finish Old Colony vase. $57-60.
Right. Satin finish Old Colony candlestick. $25-27.

Bowl, cereal, 6.38"	$27-31
Bowl, salad, 7.75"	$30-35
Bowl, plain or ribbed, 9.5"	$32-37
Bowl with three legs, 10.5"	$265-285
Candy jar and cover, ribbed	$52-54
Compote, 7"	$30-32
Compote and cover, footed	$52-57
Creamer	$26-29
Cup	$27-30
Flower bowl with crystal frog	$27-30
Plate, salad, 7.25"	$28-31
Plate, luncheon, 8.75"	$26-29
Plate, dinner, 10.5"	$35-38
Plate, grill, 10.5"	$25-29
Plate, with solid lace, 13"	$58-64
Platter, 12.75"	$40-45
Platter, five-part, 12.75"	$37-40
Relish, three part, 7.5"	$72-75
Saucer	$14-16
Sherbet	$112-119
Sugar	$26-28
Tumbler, 9 oz., flat, 4.5"	$22-24
Tumbler, 10.5 oz., footed, 5"	$87-93

Oyster and Pearl

Made by Anchor Hocking Glass from 1938 to 1940.

Bowl, round or handled, 5.25"	$14-16
Bowl, heart-shaped, one-handled, 5.25"	$12-14
Bowl, fruit, 10.25"	$27-30
Candleholder, pair, 3.5"	$27-30
Plate, sandwich, 13.5"	$22-25
Relish dish, oblong, 10.25"	$16-18

Petalware

Made by MacBeth-Evans Glass Company from 1930 to 1940.

Bowl, cream soup, 4.5"	$14-16
Bowl, cereal, 5.75"	$13-15
Bowl, large berry	$22-25
Cup	$9-11
Creamer	$10-12
Plate, sherbet, 6"	$4-6
Plate, salad, 8"	$7-9
Plate, dinner, 9"	$16-18
Plate, salver, 11"	$17-19
Platter, oval, 13"	$22-25
Saucer	$4-6
Sherbet, footed	$12-14
Sugar	$10-12

Princess

Made by the Hocking Glass Company from 1931 to 1935.

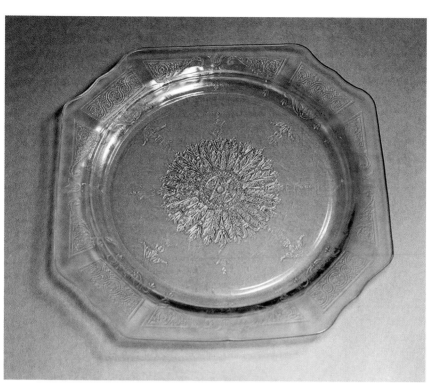

Bowl, berry, 4.5"	$27-29
Bowl, cereal, 5"	$37-42
Butter dish and cover	$95-110
Candy dish and cover	$72-76
Cookie jar and cover	$72-76
Creamer, oval	$17-19
Cup	$15-17
Plate, sherbet, 5.5"	$12-14
Plate, salad, 8"	$17-19
Plate, dinner, 9.5"	$30-35
Platter, 12"	$28-32
Sugar	$14-16
Sugar cover	$25-29
Tumbler, juice, 5 oz., 3"	$32-36
Tumbler, water, 9 oz., 4"	$27-32
Tumbler, 10 oz., footed, 5.25"	$32-36

Note: The candy dish and cover have been reproduced.

Queen Mary ("Vertical Ribbed")

Made by the Hocking Glass Company from 1936 to 1940.

Bowl, one handle or no handle, 4"	$7-9
Bowl, berry, 5"	$7-9
Bowl, cereal, 6"	$27-30
Bowl, two-handled, 5.5"	$10-12
Bowl, large berry, 8.75"	$20-22
Creamer	$12-14
Cup	$10-12
Plate, dinner, 9.75"	$55-62
Plate, sandwich, 12"	$21-25
Saucer	$4-6
Sherbet, footed	$11-13
Sugar, oval	$12-14
Tumbler, juice, 5 oz., 3.5"	$12-14
Tumbler, water, 9 oz., 4"	$17-19

Rosemary ("Dutch Rose")

Made by the Federal Glass Company from 1935 to 1937.

Bowl, berry, 5"	$10-12
Bowl, cereal, 6"	$34-38
Bowl, cream soup, 5"	$32-35
Creamer	$16-20
Cup	$10-12
Plate, dinner, 9.5"	$16-18
Plate, salad, 6.75"	$9-11
Saucer	$6-8
Sugar	$18-21

Royal Lace

Made by the Hazel-Atlas Glass Company from 1934 to 1941.

Bowl, cream soup, 4.75"	$27-29
Bowl, berry, 5"	$32-34
Bowl, round berry, 10"	$32-34
Bowl, oval vegetable, 11"	$37-39
Butter dish and cover	$155-165
Creamer, footed	$22-24
Cup	$17-19
Pitcher, 68 oz., 8"	$95-105
Pitcher, 86 oz., 8"	$127-137
Pitcher, 96 oz., 8.5"	$112-120
Plate, sherbet	$10-12
Plate, luncheon, 8.5"	$18-20
Plate, dinner, 9.88"	$32-37
Plate, oval, 13"	$40-45
Saucer	$9-11
Sugar	$17-19
Sugar lid	$45-55

Sharon ("Cabbage Rose")

Made by the Federal Glass Company from 1936 to 1939.

Bowl, berry, 5"	$15-17
Bowl, cream soup	$52-56
Bowl, cereal, 6"	$30-35
Bowl, large berry, 8.5"	$34-38
Bowl, vegetable, oval	$34-38
Butter dish and cover	$57-63
Creamer, footed	$20-22
Cup	$16-18
Plate, bread and butter, 6"	$9-12
Plate, dinner, 9.5"	$22-24
Plate, salad, 7.5"	$25-27
Platter, oval, 12.5"	$32-35
Saucer	$14-16
Sugar	$16-18
Sugar lid	$35-39

Note: Beware of the reproduction pale pink creamer and sugar, crudely made cheese dish, and salt and pepper shakers.

Sierra ("Pinwheel")

Made by the Jeannette Glass Company from 1931 to 1933.

Bowl, cereal, 5.5"	$17-19
Bowl, large berry, 8.5"	$34-38
Butter dish and cover	$67-72
Creamer	$22-24
Cup	$14-17
Pitcher, 32 oz., 6.5"	$97-105
Plate, dinner, 9"	$24-27
Platter, oval, 11"	$47-52
Salt and pepper	$42-45
Saucer	$8-11
Serving tray with handles	$20-23
Sugar	$24-27
Sugar cover	$20-24

Sunflower

Made by the Jeannette Glass Company during the late 1920s.

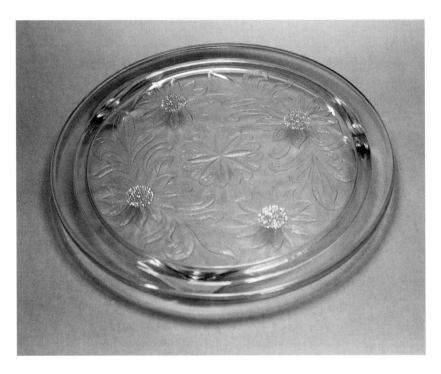

Cake plate with three legs, 10"	$17-19
Creamer	$22-24
Cup	$14-16
Plate, dinner, 9"	$20-22
Saucer	$12-14
Sugar	$22-24

Swirl ("Petal Swirl")

Made by the Jeannette Glass Company from 1937 to 1938.

Bowl, cereal, 5.25"	$13-15
Bowl, salad, 9"	$22-24
Bowl, footed with closed handles, 10"	$27-30
Candy dish, open, with three legs	$16-18
Creamer, footed	$12-14
Cup	$12-14
Plate, sherbet, 6.5"	$7-9
Plate, 7.25"	$10-12
Plate, salad, 8"	$12-14
Plate, dinner, 9.25"	$17-19
Saucer	$5-7
Tumbler, 9 oz., 4"	$22-24
Tumbler, 9 oz.	$24-26

Tea Room

Made by Indiana Glass Company from 1926 to 1931.

Creamer	$28-31
Cup	$57-62
Goblet, 9 oz.	$67-73
Pitcher, 64 oz.	$152-162
Plate, luncheon, 8.25"	$32-35

Saucer	$32-35
Sugar	$20-22
Tumbler, footed, 6 oz.	$37-42
Tumbler, footed, 9 oz.	$32-35
Tumbler, footed, 11 oz.	$47-52
Tumbler, footed, 12 oz.	$67-72

Twisted Optic

Made by the Imperial Glass Company from 1927 to 1930.

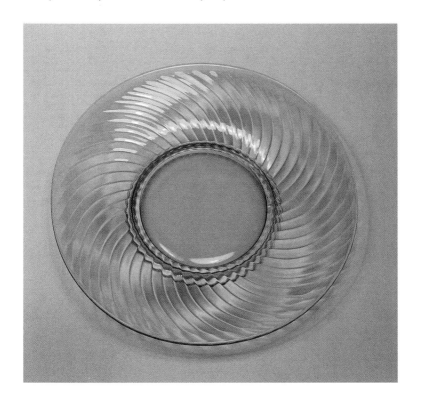

Bowl, cereal, 5"	$9-11
Bowl, soup, 7"	$14-16
Candy jar and cover	$37-40
Creamer	$11-13
Cup	$7-9
Plate, salad, 7"	$5-7
Plate, luncheon, 8"	$5-7
Sandwich server, with center handle	$24-27
Saucer	$4-6
Sugar	$8-10
Tumbler, 12 oz., 5.25"	$11-13

Waterford ("Waffle")

Made by Hocking Glass Company from 1938 to 1944.

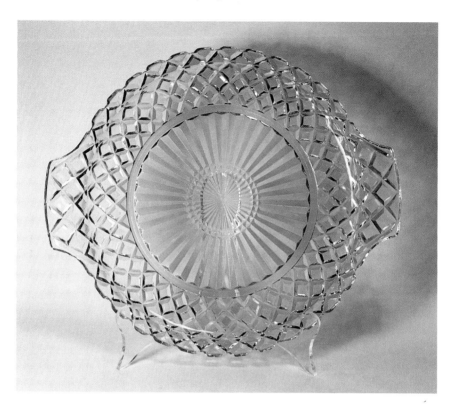

Bowl, berry, 4.75"	$20-22
Bowl, cereal, 5.5"	$37-41
Creamer, oval	$14-16
Cup	$17-19
Plate, sherbet, 6"	$9-11
Plate, dinner, 9.63"	$26-33
Plate, cake, with handles	$19-23
Saucer	$8-10
Sugar	$13-16
Sugar cover	$30-33
Tumbler, footed, 10 oz., 4.88"	$26-30

Windsor ("Windsor Diamond")

Made by the Jeannette Glass Company from 1932 to 1946.

Bowl, berry, 4.75″	$12-14
Bowl, cream soup, 5″	$23-26
Bowl, with three legs, 7.12″	$29-34
Bowl, large berry, 8.5″	$22-24
Butter dish	$49-59
Creamer	$15-17
Cup	$12-14
Pitcher, 16 oz., 4.5″	$120-130
Pitcher, 52 oz., 6.75″	$30-35
Plate, salad, 7″	$19-22
Plate, dinner, 9″	$26-30
Saucer	$5-7
Sugar and cover	$29-36
Tumbler, 5 oz., 3.25″	$27-31
Tumbler, 9 oz., 4″	$19-23
Tumbler, 12 oz., 5″	$31-36

Chapter Three: *Incidental Items*

Anchor Hocking Glass Company

Bon bon bowl. $15-17.

Tumblers. $8-10 each.

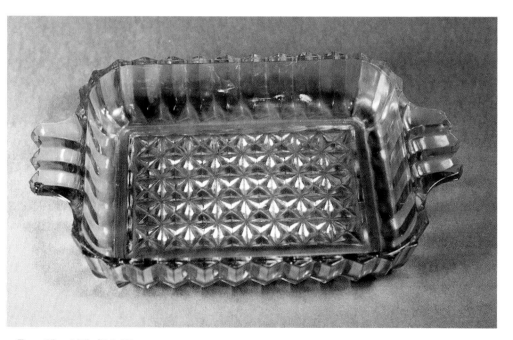

Tray, 6" x 4.5". $12-15.

Left. Sugar. $8.50-9.50.
Right. Creamer. $9.50-10.50.

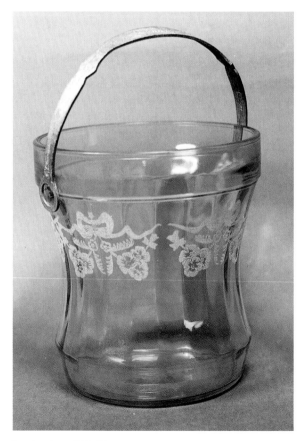

Ice bucket. $55-65.

Dessert plate. $15-17.50.

31 oz. oil lamp. $165-175.

Hand decorated sandwich plate. $45-55.

Candleholder. $20-25.

Goblet. $12.50-15.50.

Etched wine glass. $14-16.

Cambridge Glass Company

Round Dinnerware open service dish, 10.5". $45-55.

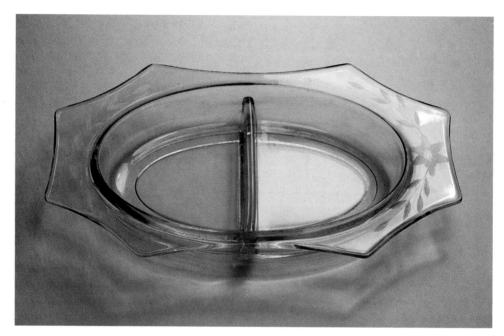

Signed etched and divided dish. $45-55.

Tray with metal base. $40-50.

Heirloom fan vase, 8.5". $35-45.

Three piece sugar and creamer set. $65-75.

Etched tumbler. $15-20.

Stand for serviette set. $25-35.

Pioneer plate. $15-25.

Cereal premium measuring cup. $25-35.

Enlarged view of inside
of measuring cup.

65 oz. jug. $65-75.

Mixing bowl. $20-30.

Diamond Lattice bowl. $18-22.

Fostoria Glass Company

Three etched dessert plates. $20-25 each.

Front. Fairfax cup. $10-12. Fairfax saucer. $8-10.
Left. Bread plate. $12-15.
Center. Salad plate. 15-18.
Right. Dinner plate. $20-22.

Three signed glasses. $12-15 each.

Footed candleholder. $30-35.

Pair of candlesticks. $90-95 for the pair.

Oval centerpiece bowl. $75-95.

Five 9 oz. tumblers. $7.50-8.50 each.

Left. Berry bowl with ruffled edges. $9-12.
Right. Large berry bowl with ruffled edges. $30-35.

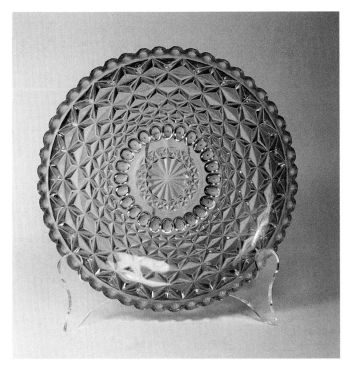

Mint tray, 7″. $18-22.

Criss Cross vase. $15-18.

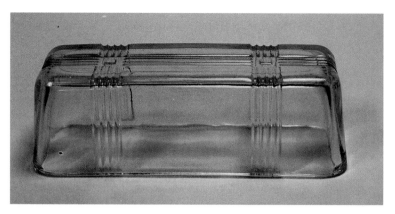

Criss Cross butter cover. $10-12.

Left and right. Diamond Optic berry bowls. $8-10 each.
Center. Large Diamond Optic berry bowl. $15-20.

Three juice glasses. $7.50-9.50 each.

Footed ice tea glass.
$12-15.

Dinner plate. $8-10.

Left and right. Four footed ice tea glasses. $8-10 each.
Center. Pitcher. $35-45.

Imperial Glass Company

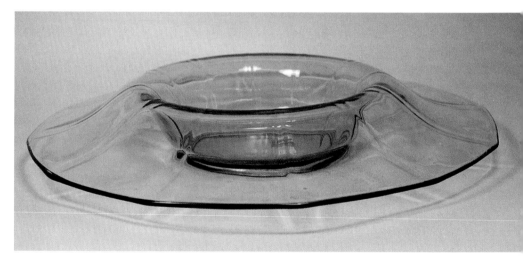

Console bowl, 11". $75-85.

Flower bowl, 11". $70-80.

Rose Marie celery tray, 10". $45-55.

Liberty Glass Company

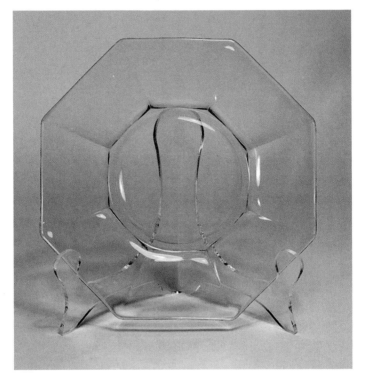

Octagon Optic dessert plate. $10-12.

MacBeth-Evans Glass Company

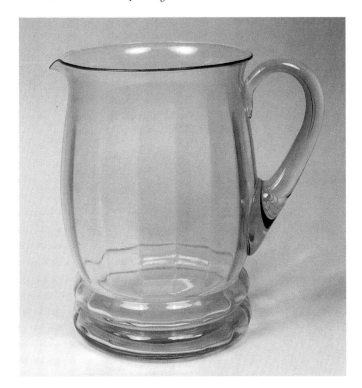

Pitcher. $55-65.

Standard Glass Company

Three etched tumblers. $9.50-10.50 each.

Mayonnaise ladle. $18-20.

Comport, 8". $65-75.

U. S. Glass Company

Eve cosmetic set holder with floral motif and figure of woman. $57-67.

Miscellaneous Items

Diamond Panel saucer. $20-30.

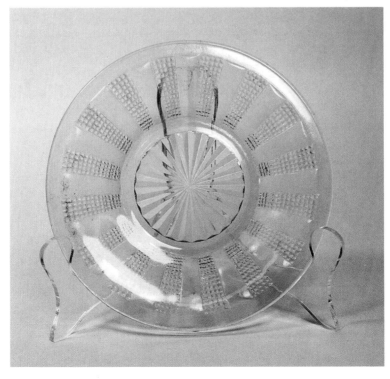

Etched bowl, 9". $55-65.

Candlestick with dolphin. $20-25.

Wine goblet, 3". $12-15.

Ring design creamer. $12-15.

Left. Tumbler. $5-7.
Right. Tumbler. $5-7.

White Hall salt and pepper shakers. $18-20 for the pair.

Bibliography

Archer, Margaret and Douglas. *Imperial Glass*. Paducah, Kentucky: Collector Books, 1990.

Brenner, Robert. *Depression Glass for Collectors*. Atglen, Pennsylvania: Schiffer Publishing, Ltd., 1998.

Cambridge Glass Company. *Fine Handmade Table Glassware*. Paducah, Kentucky: Collector Books, 1991.

Florence, Gene. *Pocket Guide to Depression Glass*. Paducah, Kentucky: Collector Books, 1999.

"The History of Anchor Hocking 1905-1996." Available from http://www.anchorhocking.com.

Kovel, Ralph and Terry. *Kovel's Depression Glass & Dinnerware Price List*. Sixth Edition. New York: Three Rivers Press, 1998.

Luckey, Carol F. *An Identification & Value Guide to Depression Era Glassware*. Florence, Alabama: Books Americana.

Measell, James and Berry Wiggins. *Great American Glass of the Roaring 20s & Depression Era*. Marietta, Ohio: The Glass Press, Inc., 1998.

Weatherman, Hazel Marie. *Colored Glassware of the Depression Era*. Springfield, Missouri: Weatherman Glassbooks, 1970.

Weatherman, Hazel Marie. *Colored Glassware of the Depression Era 2*. Springfield, Missouri: Weatherman Glassbooks, 1974.

COBALT BLUE GLASS

Monica Lynn & Patricia Rosser Clements

Glass the color of deep blue, known as cobalt blue, holds a fascination for collectors of glassware. The origin of this distinctive blue glass goes back to the Egyptians. In Cobalt Blue Glass, authors Monica Lynn Clements and Patricia Rosser Clements showcase nearly 400 photographs that illustrate the wide appeal of cobalt blue glass. From Depression Era patterns and elegant glassware to reproduction pieces and new glass, the colorful photographs exemplify what appeals to the collector. Also shown are cobalt blue glass jewelry, condiment pieces, candlesticks, vases, lamps, bells, perfume bottles, bottles and jars, animals, iridescent glass pieces, and other items. This book contains current market values. For anyone who appreciates the beauty of cobalt blue glass, this book is an indispensable reference guide.

8 1/2" x 11"	391 color photos	price guide and index
144 Pages	soft cover	$24.95	0-7643-0685-5

AN UNAUTHORIZED GUIDE TO FIRE-KING GLASSWARES
Monica Lynn Clements
& Patricia Rosser Clements
During the 1940s, the Anchor Hocking Glass Company, of Lancaster, Ohio, introduced a line known as Fire-King. This pocket-size guide offers a brief history, with over 200 full color photographs, current market values, and index. Colorful examples of dinnerware, mugs, a myriad of mixing bowls--from splash proof to Swedish Modern styles--a large selection of kitchenware, and ovenware are featured. Copper lustre, jade-ite, sapphire blue, and turquoise blue glasswares are all well represented.
6" x 9"   212 color photos   Price Guide/Index
144 Pages   soft cover $12.95   0-7643-0839-4

POCKET GUIDE TO OCCUPIED JAPAN
Monica Lynn Clements
& Patricia Rosser Clements
In Pocket Guide to Occupied Japan, authors Monica Lynn Clements and Patricia Rosser Clements showcase the wide array of products made in Japan during the American Occupation (1945–1952). Once sold in department stores or dime stores, these items are now much sought after by collectors. With a brief history and over 250 color photographs, this handheld guide features figurines, planters, vases, salt and pepper shakers, animals, toys, dishes, mugs, wall plaques, metal objects, and other interesting items made in Occupied Japan. It is a welcomed addition to anyone's personal reference library.
6" x 9"   253 color photos   price guide
160 Pages   soft cover $16.95   0-7643-0728-2

CAMEOS

Monica Lynn & Patricia Rosser Clements
This book is the first of its kind and the result of a labor of love by the authors, who researched the history of cameos and took over 500 color photographs of cameo jewelry. Over 1400 examples of cameo jewelry are depicted, representing a time span from the 1700s to the present. Subjects covered include mythological motifs of classical gods and goddesses, religious subjects and scenes, and the ever-present anonymous woman.

A history of the cameo is provided, followed by individual chapters covering each of the materials used to make cameos, including amber, amethyst, glass, jasper ware, lava, mother-of-pearl, opal, plastics, quartz, shell, topaz, and Wedgwood. The beautiful, detailed photographs show the unique artistry and design of the cameos and their settings. This extensive book and price guide will appeal to all who appreciates the cameo's timeless appeal.

8 1/2" x 11"   526 color photos
Price Guide/Index
224 Pages   hard cover $59.95
0-7643-0426-7

CAMEOS: A POCKET GUIDE

Monica Lynn & Patricia Rosser Clements
A distinctive art form appreciated since the days of Alexander the Great, cameos continue to fascinate collectors. Authors Monica Lynn Clements and Patricia Rosser Clements first showcased this fascinating subject in their book Cameos: Classical to Costume. Now they have written a companion guide, Cameos: A Pocket Guide. With over 300 color photographs, this portable guide offers a look at the beauty of finely detailed lava and shell cameos, molded cameo jewelry made from plastics, and glass, and a sampling of pieces fashioned from lesser known materials. Mythological motifs, scenes, and portraits are well represented. The book also includes a brief history of the cameo. Cameos: A Pocket Guide is a necessary addition to the personal reference library of anyone who collects cameos or simply loves the beauty of this timeless jewelry.

9" x 6"   302 color photos   price guide
160 Pages soft cover $19.95   0-7643-0737-1

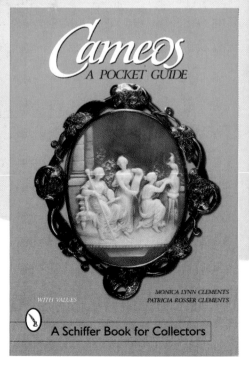